Thank you to...

My son for reminding me that the best moments happen in the present.

Eleanor Baggaley and Natacha Galbano for their work in bringing Slow Down Amaya to life.

Louise Shanagher for her teachings from The Creative Mindfulness Method.

Last but not least, to you for choosing to read Slow Down Amaya.

First Published 2024 by Snowdrop Publishing
www.Snowdrop-Publishing.com

ISBN: 978-1-916703-05-6

Copyright © Natasha Iregbu

The right of Natasha Iregbu and Natacha Galbano to be identified as the author and illustrator of this work has been asserted by them in accordance with the Copyright, Designs and Patents Act 1988.

All rights reserved. No part of this publication may be reproduced, stored in a retrieval system, or transmitted, in any form, or by any means, without the prior written permission of the author.

A CIP catalogue record for this book is available from the British Library.

SLOW DOWN
AMAYA

This book belongs to

Amaya loves to fly.

Every day she flutters from flower to flower.

Daisies, roses, tulips and daffodils.

Amaya is a busy butterfly.

Are you wondering what butterflies do all day?

Let's find out.

Amaya likes to sit on flowers, ...

... think about flowers...

... and when she goes to bed she even dreams about flowers!

One day Amaya was flying across a field and suddenly stopped.

She spotted a tall, bright sunflower. It was a very special flower.

"Wow, what a beautiful flower."

"Thank you," replied the sunflower.

"You can talk?" Amaya smiled, "I've never talked to a sunflower before."

"I-I don't speak much," stuttered the sunflower.

"That's ok. I've met other shy flowers before. My mummy told me, 'Everyone is different in their own special way.' What's your name?"

"Samuel but my mummy calls me Sammy. What's your name?"

"I'm Amaya. You look like the sun."

"Hello, Amaya. I love the sun."

"Can I come closer?"

"Yes. I know butterflies like flowers," he quietly giggled.

Amaya blushed.

Amaya smelled Sammy, "Mmmm, just like summer."

She listened to his petals blow in the wind.

She felt him, saying, "You feel so soft."

Amaya even licked him.

"Yum, yum! You taste like sweets," she exclaimed.

Amaya felt warm and fuzzy inside.

"Do you know what my favourite flower is?"

"No."

"You need to guess."

"Erm...a daisy?"

"Nope, guess again."

"Is it a rose?"

"Nope. Do you want me to tell you?"

"Yes, tell me."

"It's a sunflower!"

"Do you want to be my new friend?"

"Wow," he nodded with excitement, "I don't have many friends."

Sammy felt pleased to make a new friend.

"What is your name again?" Amaya asked.

"Sammy."

"Sorry, I forget lots of things. We can be best friends," she squealed.

Sammy smiled.

"I need to go now. I'll come and see you again tomorrow."

"Bye-bye, Amaya. I had fun playing with you today."

"I can't wait to see you again, bye Sammy!"

Amaya waved goodbye and fluttered away. She felt so happy.

Sammy watched her fly into the sky.

Do you know what Amaya was doing with Sammy when they first met?

She was practising something called mindfulness.

It's when you slow down what you are doing and pay attention to the here and now.

Practicing mindfulness means focusing on the present moment, not thinking about the past or worrying about the future.

You can practice mindfulness by using all five senses.

Come and try it with Amaya.

Hello, friend.

Close your eyes, or look towards the floor if you prefer.

Take a deep breath in through your nose while counting to 3.

1... 2... 3...

Now slowly breathe out, remember, not too fast.

Ready to start?

Look around your room.

What shapes can you see?
Can you say them out loud?

How many colours can you see? Is there anything yellow, like me?

What is touching your skin? Are you wearing something soft like my petals?

What can you smell?

What sounds can you hear? You'll need to keep quiet and listen carefully.

What can you taste?
It's ok if you can't taste anything.

Well done, you've finished your mindfulness.
How do you feel?

You can be in the here and now any time you choose.

All you need to do is remember what I did in the story.

I used my senses to...

Look. Smell. Listen. Touch and Taste.

"Oh, and I nearly forgot," Amaya remembered.

"Don't lick any flowers. You're not a butterfly!"

Where is your favourite place in nature?

Draw a picture of it below.

What kind words can you say to someone who is different from you?

What kind words would you use to describe yourself?

Go outside or look outside your window.

Draw any objects you can see that are:

Rectangle

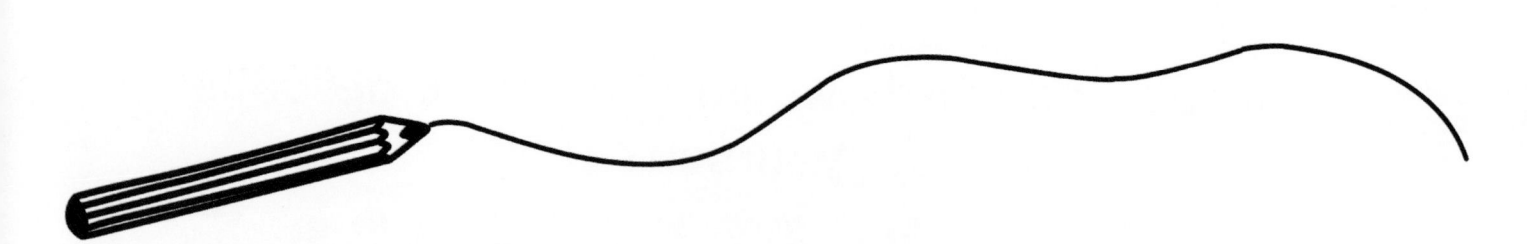

Triangle

Square

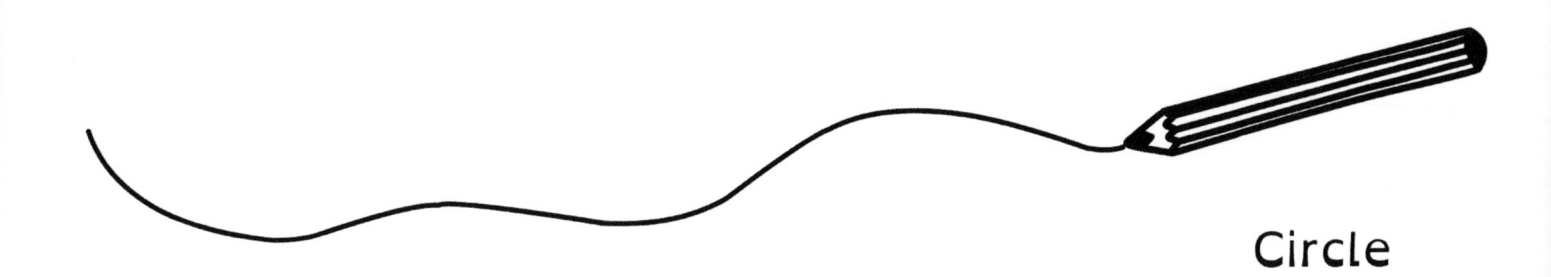

Circle

How do you feel inside your body when you are kind to someone?
Draw a picture of how you feel.

Take some deep breaths.

Place your finger on a petal and breathe in as you move your finger around the petal.

Breathe out on the next petal.

Keep going until you're back to the start.

About the Author

Natasha Iregbu is a Children's Author, Mindfulness Teacher and Coach, Yoga Teacher and Community Education Worker.

Slow Down Amaya is her debut book which shares mindfulness with children in a fun and simple way.

She used her varied experience to bring topics of diversity, inclusion, compassion and emotional literacy into *Slow Down Amaya*.

Printed in Great Britain
by Amazon